Google Classroom for Teachers

A Comprehensive Guide to Help Teachers to Set Up their Virtual Classroom and Teach Successfully

Martha Avrith

Under no circumstances will any legal responsibility or blame be held against the publisher for any reparation, damages, or monetary loss due to the information herein, either directly or indirectly.

Respective authors own all copyrights not held by the publisher.

The information herein is offered for informational purposes solely, and is universal as so. The presentation of the information is without contract or any type of guarantee assurance.

The trademarks that are used are without any consent, and the publication of the trademark is without permission or backing by the trademark owner. All trademarks and brands within this book are for clarifying purposes only and are the owned by the owners themselves, not affiliated with this document.

Table Of Contents

Introduction

Google Classroom is free of online charge service developed for schools by Google, which aims to simplify paperless formation, distribution, and grading of assignments. Google Classroom's primary aim is to streamline the mechanism by which teachers and students exchange information.

Google Classroom integrates Google Drive for making and sharing tasks, Google Docs, Writing sheets and slides, Contact Gmail, and Scheduling Google Calendar. Students can be invited via a private code to enter a college, or imported automatically from a school domain. Class creates a separate folder in the Drive of the respective individual, where the student can send work for a teacher to grade. Mobile applications, which are available for iOS and Android devices, allow users to take images and add to tasks, share files from other phones, and offline access. Teachers can track each student's progress, and teachers can return work along with feedback after grading.

Google Classroom brings together Google Drive, Google Docs, Sheets, Slides, and Gmail to help educational institutions transition to a paperless system.

Google Calendar was later incorporated to help with due task dates, field trips, and speaking classes. Students can be invited to classrooms via the institution's database, via a private application that can then be added to the student's user interface or imported automatically from a school domain. Every class created with Google Classroom creates a separate folder in the Google Drive for the respective user, where the student can send work for a teacher to grade. Tasks are stored and graded on Google's suite of productivity applications that enable the student to interact with the teacher and the student or student. Instead of exchanging documents that reside with the instructor on the student's Google Drive, files are stored on the student's computer, and submitted for grading. Students can also opt to attach additional documents to the assignment from their Drive. Google Classroom supports various grading schemes. Teachers have the option to add files that students can access, edit, or get an individual copy to the assignment. Students are able to create files and then add them to the assignment if the instructor has not made a copy of a file. Teachers have the opportunity to track each student's progress towards the assignment where they can comment and edit. The instructor will rate the turned in assignments and return them with feedback to encourage the student to update the assignment and return. When marked, the teacher can only edit assignments until the instructor hands the assignment back in. Teachers can post advertisements to the class stream, which students can comment on, enabling two-way contact between the teacher and the students. Students can still post to the class stream, but a teacher's announcement would not be as high as a priority and can be moderated. Google products can attach multiple types of media, such as YouTube videos and Google Drive files, to announcements and posts to share content. Gmail also provides teachers email options to send emails to one or more students inside the Google Classroom app. You can access the Classroom on the web or through the mobile devices Android and iOS Classroom.

Chapter 1: Google Classroom and its uses

1.1 What is Google Classroom?

Google describes Google School as "The school mission control," and that could be the best way to think about it. Simply put, it's a forum for teachers and students to connect Google's G Suite resources. This also serves as a multimedia organizer where teachers can hold and exchange class materials with students — all of them paperless. In there, you can select which features you wish to implement. This simplicity, and its seamless integration with the popular Google tools, is possibly what has made Google Classroom one of today's most commonly used edtech tools. Google Learning helps teachers to create an online classroom environment where they will be able to access all the information their students need. Documents are stored on Google Drive and editable for applications such as Google Docs, Tickets, etc. But what distinguishes Google Classroom from the standard Google Drive experience is the interface between teacher and student, developed by Google for the way teachers and students think and work.

Google Classroom is a free Google created program. The platform helps communicate with teachers and students and can be used to coordinate and manage to learn. Google Classroom is considered an essential paperless teaching aid to help teachers and students collaborate. The software also allows teachers to teach from a distance and can provide much-needed support in the current environment. This is part of the Google Apps for Education series that aims to make paperless learning possible in the Classroom.

Google Classroom is a free program for teachers and learners to collaborate. Teachers can create classes online, invite students to attend the class, and create and hand out assignments. Inside the forum, learners and teachers can interact with the assignments, and teachers can track the progress of students. To use this solution, schools can create a free Google Apps for Education account.

Google Classroom offers teachers and students special features that are not part of traditional Google Accounts. For example, teachers may use the Formulas tool to add images and answers to questions with multiple choices.

The Gmail Inbox app houses Classroom texts, allowing students and teachers to find highlights and main information with ease. By adding subjects to posts, teachers can coordinate their class streams, and students and teachers can search the streams to find different subjects. Google Classroom is perfect for parents too. Teachers can exchange student success summaries with their parents, and the latter can get automatic email summaries of class updates and student assignments.

1.2 Who can use Google Classroom?

Anybody! Google Classroom is a free service for those with a Google personal account, and it is also open for organizations that use G Suite for Education or G Suite for Nonprofits. In most cases, teachers and students can use a Google account offered by their school to access Google Classroom. Although the primary users of Google Classroom are teachers and students in classrooms, there are also features that administrators, families, and homeschoolers can use. One of the first things you should do as an teacher in the Classroom is to create a class for each of the classes you are teaching.

In a class, students can be assigned work and post announcements. Anyone over 13 can use a personal Google Account to build the class. Unless your school does have a G Suite for Education account, however, you can use that email to build your classes.

For info, go to User Accounts in the Classroom. Teachers have been switching online classes because of the coronavirus pandemic as schools, colleges, and universities closed campuses.

This transition tested the willingness of many teachers to adapt content and practices during the pandemic while at home-often with other family members. Fortunately, schools using G Suite have access to Google Classroom, a cloud-based system that helps teachers create and manage courses, classwork, grades, and student communication. Google also created a new program, Teach from Home, in response to the COVID-19 crisis explicitly designed to help teachers adapt to online courses. The website offers links to tutorials to help teachers develop experience with different G Suite teaching resources. The following tips are intended as an add-on, based on many years of online platform teaching.

1. Google Classroom supports sequenced learning for anyone

Especially during a period of remote-only work, Google Classroom will support learning needs for all sorts of organizations along with G Suite apps. Google Classroom may be used by any company that uses G Suite: it is not restricted to schools. The classroom allows a viable choice to help a teacher lead any group of individuals through a set of organized topics and tasks. While a teacher with a collection of students will always use the Classroom, the same method will also be used for professional development efforts.

2. Understand context

Cellular telephones and personal digital assistants (PDAs)-such as Blackberry, Smartphone, and Treo devices-allow fast communications, remote wireless network access, and more efficient mobile employees. These tools do contribute significantly, however. When you attempt to express information, aim to understand the student context. Students may face difficulties not usually present in a school classroom, including in-household children of certain ages, adults who may also be home, and a physical setting not generally structured to facilitate learning. To the degree practicable, take the time to make sure every one of your students understands the meaning and circumstances.

3. Enable offline work

Change assignments to encourage students to work offline, as not every home student will have access to an internet connection. Statistics by Pew Research indicate that "15% of U.S. households with school-age children do not have high-speed internet service at home." Provide access to materials that can be downloaded, rather than downloading.

You could, for example, record a video (e.g., with Hangouts Meet) then upload it to Google Classroom instead of linking it to a YouTube video. Likewise, instead of a web connection, you might include an article that you want students to read as a PDF or Google Doc. Explore an EPUB version if you intend to teach with a very long text, which allows the reader more control over fonts, and line spacing and font size. A student can download and store items to Google Drive for offline access, including a PDF, video file, or Google Docs, Sheets, or Slides.

4. Verify that a mobile app can perform an assignment

Ideally, you'd also check to make sure any task can be done on an Android phone, iPhone, or laptop in Chrome. For instance, most assignments involving the use of Google Docs, Papers, or Slides will work well, as those apps not only work well in a browser but can also be installed on Android and iOS devices. The Docs, Boards, and Slides apps currently differ slightly by the platform. Support for add-ons (in Docs, Sheets, and Slides), drop-down lists (in Google Sheets), and audio or video files inserted (in Google Slides), for example, vary. In every G Suite app on Android, iOS, or Chrome on the web, not every feature functions the same way, so it helps check new assignments and tasks.

If you don't have access to the three platforms checking your assignment (i.e., Android, iOS, Chrome), contact the tech support team at your school. A well-run IT support department is likely to be able to arrange a time to help you check that any device can complete a task. Even if your organization provides students with a computer, I urge you to create platform-neutral assignments to optimize the students' ability to complete a mission, regardless of the system. Recall always testing assignments for any third-party applications that you are using.

5. Join the conversation on Twitter

Google encourages people to use the hashtag # teach from home, but there are also many excellent tools for other hashtags, including # distance learning, # edtech, # remote learning, and # mobile learning.

1.3 Google Classroom's Usage by Educators

Since it is a relatively versatile platform, educators take advantage of its functionality in several different ways. Teachers can: Streamline how they handle classes with Google Classroom. The platform integrates with other tools such as Files, Drive, and Calendar from Google, and there are plenty of built-in "shortcuts" for classroom management tasks. For example, If you file a due date report, your students will automatically see it added to the class calendar. Google Classroom lets you build a special class for each class you're teaching. You can build a class in just three mouse clicks and a few keystrokes. Google Classrooms are broken up into different parts. You will show all of the students in your class in section Classes. You can either manually add students to your class, or you can use your own Google account to enter your class by yourself.

When designing a class, Google Classroom provides you with a class code located on the left side of the screen. Share the class code with the students that you'd like to enter. Students sign into their Google Accounts from their phones, tablets, or Chrome books and use the class code to enter.

You will also decide within the Student section whether your students can comment on the comments, announcements, and assignments you are making or whether they can only post. If you wish, you can also choose to be the only one in your class who can post and comment.

You'll find the tasks, announcements, and questions you generate in the Stream section. This is the area you'll be spending most of your time after setting up your classes. Read below for information on Google Classroom assignments, questions, and announcements. Assignments are a perfect way to collect student work and offer reviews and grades to the students. When you make an assignment, you should include detailed instructions, due dates, and a subject for that assignment. If you have a due date for the assignment, the students will have to apply their work for that assignment before 11:59 PM on the day. If they send the job late, the task is still approved by Google Classroom, but it means that it was turned in late.

Google Classroom Assignments, one of the best features, is that you can add files to the assignments you make. You should connect a link to your Desktop, a Google Drive file, a video from YouTube, or a link to a Website.

One concept is that a teacher in business education may give a written prompt to a particular person in the news and add a link to that individual's YouTube video delivering a speech. Students can upload files of any kind to your Classroom, not just to Google Docs. Not only can students upload their completed work as files, but you can open and grade them directly from the Classroom right there. You can access data that are sent to your Classroom as long as your computer has an Internet connection and the program required to open the file. you don't even need to be on your school computer. For instance, you can assign an essay, and your students can submit their completed articles from any computer which has a Internet connection to an assignment you created in your Google Classroom. You can then open the file at school or home, and store it on your computer. Google Classroom for tasks functions like a "Dropbox." Students don't have to print their work anymore and hand it directly to you. This gives you more time to concentrate on going forward during training, as opposed to wasting time gathering research.

Organize, distribute, and compile assignments, materials for the course, and student research online. Teachers are often able to post an assignment to different classes or to change and repeat assignments year after year.

Google Classroom will help you avoid any trips to the photocopier and cut down on some of the paper shufflings that come with teaching and learning if your students have daily access to the tools.

Communicate about your classwork with the others. You may use the website to post warnings and assignment notes, and it is easy to see who has finished their job or who has not. You may also check-in privately with individual students, answer their questions, and provide support. Within a given class, Google Classroom allows you to ask a question. You should add files to your inquiries, as with assignments, and you can apply a due date if you wish. In the Classroom, you can post short answer questions or multiple choice questions for your students to answer. As students answer a question of numerous choices, Google Classroom tabulates the results for that question and shows you the breakdown in real-time of the answers from the students. When you click on one of the answers to multiple choices, the Classroom will indicate which students have chosen that option.

If students answer a short answer question, the answers cannot be tabulated by Google Classroom, so it simply displays responses from the students.

You can comment or respond to each student at that level, and give them a grade as you see fit. Google Classroom helps you to make announcements, in addition to creating tasks and questions. Students can respond to your announcements and, by creating a line, you can answer back. The whole class can have one announcement based conversation. Again you have the option to add an announcement file, a YouTube video, or a connection. Advertisements are a perfect way to post updates to the students about assignment due dates. You can also plan to post updates at a later date, which will help you and your students remain organized. Offer timely feedback to the students on their assignments and assessments. Google Forms can be used inside Google Classroom to build and exchange quizzes, which are automatically graded as students turn them in. Not only do you spend less time grading, but your students will provide instant feedback on their work.

Chapter 2: Setting Up Google Classroom and Using Other Apps with it

2.1 Setting Google Classroom in Simple Steps

You should find it easy to set up and very natural to continue to use it. Follow those steps to set up your teacher account at Google Classroom:

1. Sign up

You can use the Classroom by logging in using a G suite e-mail address when you go to classroom website, or you can use it for educational purposes without a "text." That way, everything works just fine too.

If you have hundreds of them, it's only harder to handle your pupils. You're going to have to add that one by one. Through downloading the Google Classroom app, and entering your account information, You may sign in as a teacher or student to a Google Classroom session. Please notice that your school must be registered with Google Apps for Education account for you to have access to Google Classroom; you must also be signed in to Google Chrome with your school email credentials. On Google Chrome, open a blank tab. If you're not running Google Chrome on your machine, you can download it from any other web browser for free. Click on the top right corner of the "Men" page. It is just to the left of the "Minimize" button, which appears like a person's outline. If anyone is already signed into Chrome, then it lists their name. Click the button to "Sign in to Chrome." If somebody's already signed in to Chrome, then press "Move User." Type the Gmail address in your grade, then press "Next." Note, this cannot be your email account as Google Classroom is accessible only through an email address that is connected to the school. The school's address will look like "myname@myschool.edu." Type your password in. Click "Sign in" to log those credentials into Chrome. It will carry you back to the blank page you started on. Use the Google Classroom app to navigate. Note, to log in to the Classroom you need to have an email address from the school.

Google

Sign in to Chrome

Sign in with your Google Account to get your bookmarks, history, passwords and other settings on all your devices

Email or phone

Forgot email?

Not your computer? Use Guest mode to sign in privately. Learn more

Create account   Next

English (United Kingdom)   Help   Privacy   Terms

If you are a student, enter your code for the exam. Until class starts, your instructor should have equipped you with this. To enter the classroom please presses "Enter." You signed up for Google Classroom with results. Sign up for Google Education Apps Open a blank page inside Google Chrome.

To access Google Classroom, you will need to register the website details of your school — also known as a "domain" — with Google Apps for Education, which is software of frees teacher instructional aids and devices. Navigate to the Google Education Applications website. Tap at the bottom of the page under "Download Google Apps for Learning." In the middle of the screen is a large blue circle. This will take you to the development page for the account. Click on the "Start" button in blue. It's next to the choice "Order from our Website." In the popup window, embrace or decline partner support. Clicking on the grey "I will need some help" button will support you in the process, while the blue "Got it" button will allow you to set up your account. Click on the pop-up window to "yeah, let's get started." To set up Google Apps for Education, you will have access to the web domain of your school so make sure that you have the knowledge readily accessible.

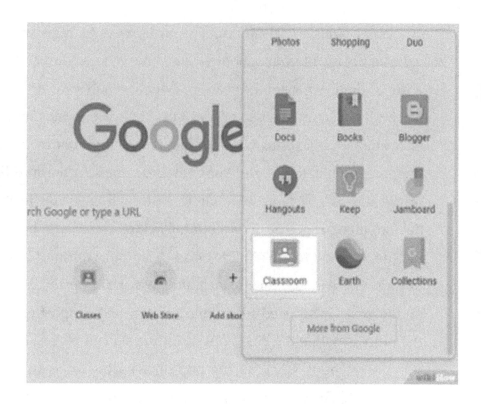

2. Create your first class

In your computer upper right corner, click on the "+" button. Select "Form a Group" You fill in some info about your class here. Write down a name and section of a strong college. The name of the class will be your class title so that you can find it back in a few seconds. Then press the Build button.

Google Learning helps teachers to create an online classroom environment where they will be able to access all the information their students need. Teachers can make assignments from inside the class that their students complete and turn in for gradation.

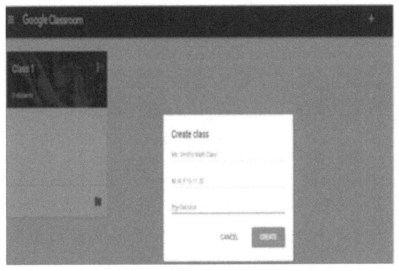

To build a class, follow these steps: open a web browser and go to the website of the school. You will sign in to your account with Google Apps for Education.

Tap the plus sign at the top on the Welcome screen, and select Build Class.

Type the Class Name and Section into the Build a Class dialog box.

Click on the Create button.

You are building your new classroom. You can see that there are three key tabs in the classroom.

Stream: This is where you're handling your class assignments and making class announcements. You may add new assignments, with due dates and materials attached.

Students: It is where the students are treated. From here you can invite students into your classroom and handle their level of permissions. To invite students to your class, you must set them up in your Google Apps for Education account as Google Contacts, or they must be on the school list.

About: This is where you can add the title and description of the course, add a place for the class and attach materials to the Google Drive folder for your lesson. Once you build at least one class, when you sign in you will no longer see the Welcome screen.

You see the Home screen instead. This screen shows all groups grouped in tiles. To use it simply click on the name of the class. Below are a few other features of the Home screen: Add a new class: Just like you can add a new class on the Welcome page, by clicking on the plus sign next to your username in the upper left.

Rename or archive a class: To either rename or archive the class, click on the three stacked dots next to the class name. Archiving a class ensures that while you and your students are still able to access the class, no one is allowed to add assignments or make any other adjustments. Under the Archived portion of the Home menu, the class must pass. But don't worry; you can restore the archived class by browsing Archived Classes at any time, click the three stacked dots, and selecting Restore.

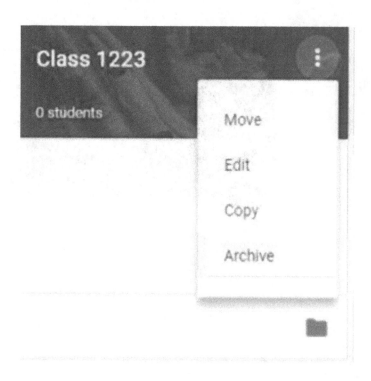

For the class, access Google Drive: Press the file folder icon in the class tile's bottom right corner. This opens the Google Drive, where all resources in your classroom are stored.

3. Invite students to your class

You can then invite your students once you have built your class. Let them register by entering the unique code you've given them using the Google Classroom app. You can find the code in your class which was developed. Go to the "students" 'page. Another choice is to allow your students to enter their e-mail address, one by one. One thing you should keep in mind: your students need an e-mail address from Gmail or Google. You can also visit classroom website to let your students go. You can select "join class" there, enter the class code, and you are in! This might be a little easier because you don't have to type in the e-mail address of every student. Now ready for your online lesson! At least, it's there, and it's open to everyone. You have to do a few other things before you can take off for good.

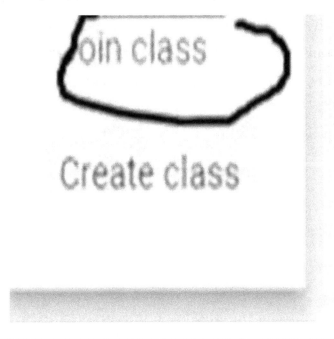

Build your first task or advertise. In the path, you can share the first announcement or go to Classwork-click on the "+ Build" button and send your first assignment to Google Classroom. Don't forget to have your assignments counted. Your students will find it easier to see which one comes first as you can't reorder assignments in the stream. You can, however, transfer assignments up to the top. Click on the title to see if there are any students in the assignment, and to give grades and feedback. You should then return the assignments to your students so that they can start editing again.

Connect some lesson material to your class/task. Fill in Google Drive material or add a YouTube video, a computer file, a connection, etc. You will find those options right below the due date. If you just want to share your class presentation, which is not related to an assignment, you can go to the "About" tab. A few lesson materials like slides, interesting papers, and examples can be added here.

Open the folder on Drive. Each time a new class is created. For that class, Google Classroom builds a Drive folder. In your class, you can navigate the folder by going to all tiles. You can find a folder icon on each piece of tile. Click on it in the folder you are. You can add materials for the class here too. Both the assignments of your students will eventually end up in the Google Drive tab, and you can find it back whenever you wish. And the most relevant issue is possibly this. Why should you use a Classroom on Google? What do you think is in it? You can get started after you have configured your classroom. In a few minutes, you'll find out how to set up your Google Classroom account. Let me first show you why Google Classroom's a big deal.

Add announcements and lesson material: give announcements about your lesson to your students. The announcements include the lesson materials. These announcements will appear in the Google Classroom stream of your students. That way, the students can easily find anything. You can attach materials from a Google drive, connect to the lesson in Google Classroom, attach files and pictures from your phone, add a YouTube video, or add some other connection that your students want to see. That is so simple!

Add assignments: You can add an assignment to your course just as you add an announcement. It works the same way, but you get the option of adding a due date and scoring it here. When they have to make an assignment, it will alert the students, and it will also appear in their calendar. You can also add an assignment to the BookWidgets in just a few minutes.

For Ms. Smith's Math Class M, W, F 10-11.30 ▾   All students ▾

Title

Assignment 001

Instructions (optional)

Write a 1 page introduction on yourself

Points 20   ▾   Due No due date ▾   Topic No topic   ▾

Saved   ASSIGN ▾

Degree an assignment: You can then review and rate the assignments your students have given in. There's space for input through a comment from an instructor. Then, return the task to your students. The "Marks" tab holds a grade book of the assignments and grades of your students.

Manage students: The students will, of course, be able to share their thoughts. Or don't they? That is entirely up to you! You can handle permissions, allow students to post and comment, comment only, or grant the teacher the right to post and comment only. And the students can be e-mailed individually.

2.2 Apps to Use for Resources for Google Classroom.

With a link to the web site or page, you can add practically everything to Google Classroom. Google Classroom has a lot of apps that have a built-in sharing feature. Students can thus easily open the app via Google Classroom.

Here's what you need to do: build an application or website account.

Build an activity or tool inside the program or web site for your students.

Use the option "transfer to Classroom." You can find the option in the application somewhere.

Now you can do stuff like create a quiz, and allocate it in one of your classes to your students.

1. BookWidgets

With BookWidgets, you can create immersive workouts on tablets, computers, and smartphones for your students. As an instructor, you can choose between over 40 different games and exercises.

We'll send you the template; in just a few clicks, you'll add your idea for a lesson. That is so simple! Students use their iPod, Chrome book, or smartphone to open the exercise using a special short code or to scan the QR code you gave them. And, in Google Classroom immediately, you can only give them a BookWidgets exercise. Simply download the Chrome plugin BookWidgets and get started in Google Classroom. With the Live widget feature, you can also follow the operation of your students, live, from a distance, inside Google Classroom. BookWidgets 'greatest benefit is that it's so diverse.

2. EDpuzzle

EDpuzzle is an inexpensive and simple way to deliver videos in your (Google) Classroom. And it is not just a distributor of videos. Connect audio-notes and video questions. EDpuzzle makes adding comments to videos simple, and the questions make the video interactive. When do you use EDpuzzle? When students watch a video, you can use it to encourage critical thinking. It is perfect for flipped classes, too.

3. Buncee

Buncee is a design and presentation tool that allows the production of material for all classroom purposes simple for you and your students. You can make an excellent presentation, an interactive novel, an entertaining lesson, or a lovely card. Buncee has a lot of fun and interactive media tools and graphics that make it more visual and enjoyable to show. In Google Classroom, add a slideshow, made with Buncee, to your class materials. Students will visit and use the presentation to review a test, or do homework.

4. Nearpod

Nearpod is like Buncee, a presentation device too. It is a lot more than that too! Make your own immersive introductions. Attach some slides, slide by slide, or pick a specific Sway template that you can change. Each of those slides makes a great interactive presentation. Especially when you're adding activities such as quizzes, open-ended questions, surveys, questions are drawing, and others. Inside your talk, what about taking your students on a field trip? Only add a slide from Nearpod's library featuring a virtual reality experience. Your students can choose to enter a code in their Nearpod app or just click on the connection in Google Classroom assigned to them. When your presentation is ready, you are in charge of the presentation as an instructor. If you turn to another slide, the students 'presentation tools will turn to that slide as well. If your students have to do a quiz or questionnaire, they should do it on their computer, as it's part of the presentation. A live set of responses! So, you can see what your students react immediately.

5. Screencastify

If you want to provide simple online instructions, enabling students to process learning material at their own speed, you can use Screencastify to record your screen, speech, and yourself while offering instructions and guidance to students from a distance through some learning materials. Think of homework, or whether certain students need homeschooling and you're teaching them from a Google Classroom distance. Screencastify makes the development of instruction videos super-easy. Simply install your Chrome browser's Screencastify app, and start making videos by recording your screen and voice. Students will follow through on-screen step while listening to your comments. Upon completion, save and import the video and share it in your learning environment (e.g., Google Classroom) with your students.

6. Newsela

Newsela develops an understanding of reading through graded posts, real-time appraisals, and actionable insights. Students are able to read papers at their own rate. Newsela delivers stories on five adaptive read rates from world-class news publications.

Embedded tests such as quizzes can also unlock improvement. So, you can include any of these articles in Google Classroom if you need a good text that's suited to different read rates.

7. Quizlet

Quizlet is a survey tool tailored to words and meanings. You add a class as a coach and take a quiz. Share this quiz with only a few clicks on your Google Classroom. They just have to click on the Google Classroom assignment and select which game they want to play in. They can take a test, select the learning mode, learn by flashcards or match words to their meanings. Quizlet Live helps the students to work together to find the correct term or meaning for the description. It is designed for the analysis of descriptions and terms. There's a tough thing, though: you can't see what your teammates are saying. If anyone makes a mistake on your squad, you need to start over again. Teams are challenging each other to be the first team to cross the finish line.

Chapter 3: Tips and Tricks for Teachers to Use Google Classroom

3.1 Six Great Google Classroom Tips for Teachers

Google Classroom is popular with teachers nationwide and is continually being updated. That's why we decided to share with your students an actual list of useful ways you can use the site. So, whether you're using Classroom at the moment or just exploring, read through the list below and consider how these features could work. Want to keep posted on new releases and changes of features? Try this useful tool to find out every month what's new in the Classroom.

1. Communicate with parents and guardians.

You may invite parents to sign up for a regular or weekly email rundown on what's happening in classes for their children. The emails contain pending or missed assignments for a student, as well as updates and queries that you have received in the class stream.

2. Help students stay organized with Google Calendar.

For each lesson, Classroom automatically generates a Google Calendar and updates the calendar with future research and due dates for the students.

Students will see things such as study days and field trips, too. The view of the calendar makes it easier to keep on track. Because new assignments or altered due dates automatically synchronize, students still see the most up-to-date material.

3. Assign work to a subset of students

Teachers may delegate individual students or a group of students within a class to work and post announcements. This feature helps teachers to separate instruction as needed, as well as support group work in collaboration. To find out how this works, check out our picture below.

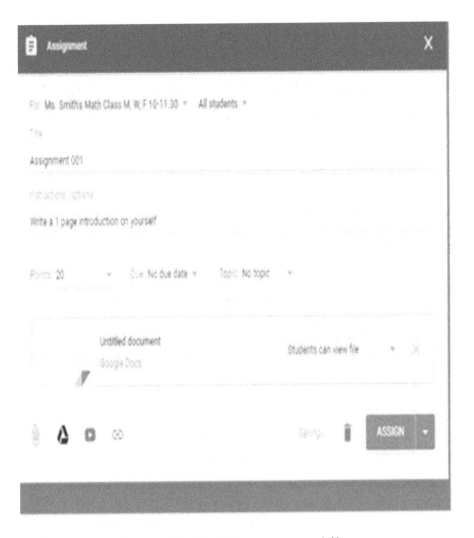

4. Use annotations with the Classroom mobile app.

Students and teachers can use the Classroom software on mobile devices running Android, iOS, and Chrome. By annotating student research in the App, you can provide real-time feedback. Students may also annotate their assignments to convey an idea or concept with greater ease.

5. Explore Classroom integrations with other tools.

Google Classroom uses an API to communicate with and share all of your favorite resources. It combines hundreds of applications and websites, including Pear Table, Actively Know, Newsela, and many, many more. Should you wish to find out more, check out our post about Google Classroom-integrated applications and websites?

6. Encourage administrators to use Classroom metrics.

Although this feature is still worth noting here for administrators — not students, administrators may use the Admin console to display statistics such as how many classes were created, how many posts were posted, and the teachers are using the tool. Access to this knowledge will help in tailoring teacher support.

Another 15 Google Classroom Tips for Teachers

1. Number your assignments!

Numbering your tasks is one of the best tips that I have ever received. It allows you not only to arrange files in the Classroom but also to keep Google Drive smooth and tidy.

2. Use Cntrl + F to Find Numbers and Words in Classroom

After a few weeks of assignments, even the most structured Classwork page can get very long. To check for keywords or assignment numbers (as mentioned above) on the tab, use the keyboard shortcut, Control + F. Teach the trick to students, too!

3. Pick an Organizational Strategy for Using Topics

Using the topics feature on the classroom page helps coordinate student and instructor assignments. There are many different ways to organize yourself. There are many ways this can be achieved, and what works for one teacher doesn't work for another. To teachers, this is a personal choice. Pick a technique that works for your region and grade level of content. Check out this article on How to Organize Assignments at Google Classroom for ideas.

4. Create a "Resources" Topic and Keep at the Top of the Classwork Page

That class requires a place to store resources, connections, rules, of course, syllabus, and so on. Mindy Barron recommends that you build a unique resource and class material subject, and keep it close to the top for easy access. Ensure sure these files are simply called, so students know exactly what's in there.

5. Create a Google Classroom Class Template

When you have selected your preferred form of organizing for Google Classroom (and checked it!), make a copy of the class as your example. You can keep creating a copy anytime you need a new class and have all of your topics already produced and arranged, and your assignments will be saved as drafts!

To make a copy of a class in Google Classroom: go to your Google Classroom account, then click on the class card's three dots and select "copy class." For more comprehensive instructions and tips on this concept, go to Google Classroom's How to create a class template.

6. Use Direct Links to Assignments

Knew, you might have a direct connection to a particular assignment? This makes referring students back to a given activity so simple. Just go to the Classwork tab, locate the assignment, right-click on the three dots, and copy the document.

7. Use a Google Doc as a Syllabus

Most teachers use Google Docs to create a syllabus so that it can be revised during the year as a living text. Add connections to external services, regular allocations, essential dates, etc.

You can also place links to Google Classroom assignments (see above) to prevent students from being checked too long.

8. Break Projects into Smaller Assignments with Separate Due Dates

Project-based learning is so important, and when we continue to push beyond the stagnant, one-and-done tasks, we need to think differently about how we put this into action in our classrooms. For students, big projects can be daunting, particularly those who haven't learned how to manage their time. Giving them milestones and splitting the project into smaller assignments with checkpoints is crucial. In reality, that's one of my book's implementing tips, Shake up Learning: Practical Ideas for Shifting Learning from Static to Dynamic.

9. Create a Separate Class for Enrichment and Extension Activities

In my class, early completion of your assignment didn't mean either free time or games. It has included reading and learning programs for my pupils. Consider having a separate class for extension or enrichment programs within Google Classroom. You might also gamify the concept and offer digital badges to accomplish a challenge or mission.

10. Use Private Comments for Meaningful Feedback and Conversations with Students

One of my Google Classroom favorite features is the private comment app. This little tool will help streamline communication and boost the feedback loop with your students. Teacher feedback is one of the main factors for student development! Personal remarks between you and your student are just that – own. (No one else will read it.) Remember to use private comments not only at the end of the task but all over! So this doesn't negate the influence of face-to-face meetings, but it does help record so that students can remember the feedback, as well as allow students to connect who don't usually speak in front of the class. There are many places where students can add private feedback. To add a private comment from the Student Work page: Click on the assignment on which you want to receive input from the Classwork tab. Click on the "View Task" button. Select the student from the left-hand roster. You can see "Add Private Comment" at the bottom of the right-hand column. Click to type in and submit your student's private comment. You can now also add private comments from inside the student's document using the latest grading feature in Google Classroom.

Click the assignment you would like to provide feedback from the Classwork tab. Click the "View Task" tab. Click the student file you want to give input on. To make a private message, use the panel at the top.

11. Use Private Comments for Reflection

Some teachers take the private comments feature a step further and make it part of the assignment by requiring that students add a reflection as a private comment after they submit their job. Sean Fahey suggests using an open-ended question or gives students a prompt like, "What did you like most about the assignment?" or "What part challenged you the most?"

12. Attach a Template Document for Each Assignment.

You can view the assignment page in Google Classroom, and see a thumbnail for each student. That allows you to see change at a glance or lack of it. Even if you don't have a template for your task, that you add a saved black document as a reference so you can still get a glimpse of the thumbnails!

13. Invite Teachers that are Hesitant to Use Google Classroom to Be a Student or Co-Teacher in Your Class.

At first, I recommend welcoming them as a guest, so they get an understanding of how this works before they can incorporate and edit the class as a co-teacher. Within a class, co-teachers can do anything you want. They are inviting students. Click on the invite teacher's icon to welcome you as a co-teacher and type in your name or email address and press Invite. Click the Invite Students icon to invite an instructor as a student and type in their name or email address and then press invite.

14. Create a demo student account to demonstrate Google Classroom to your students.

Currently, Google Classroom does not give teachers a way to view their classes as a student. And you must have a student account to view your class as a student. A solution suggested by Julie Sweeney Newton is to use a sample account and sign in as a student to see how the classroom side works and to demonstrate how to use the Classroom for your students. It is simple if you have access to build Google Accounts in the domain of your school. That kind of access is not open to most teachers. In this case, contact the tech coach or tech support to see whether a trial account can be accessed.

15. Package your Digital Assignments

This guide is a series of tips to maximize how students will need your directions and bundle it into their Google Classroom assignments.

Here are tips that will save you time and safeguard your safety.

The more information you provide in the task, the fewer questions you need to answer, and the fewer reasons students have for failing to complete the task and on time.

3.2 Google Classroom and Differentiated Support for Students

Google Classroom may help streamline the formative assessment, which is essential to benefit students who may need more support or additional challenges. For example, you can easily create, distribute, and collect digital exit tickets or auto-graded appraisals using the platform. Google Classroom can, in a way, make it easier and faster to gather daily feedback on the progress of your students. There are, of course, plenty of other formative evaluation resources out there, many of which now provide Google Classroom integrations.

Google Classroom also makes it easy for individual students or small groups to customize assignments. This means teachers will give other students or groups in a class changed or different assignments. You also have the opportunity to check-in privately with a student and see if they have questions or need any extra support. The ability to do all of this online may make the distinction efforts of teachers less visible for the class, something that could be beneficial to students who might feel singled out. Differentiation will still be a matter of innovative problem-solving with or without a resource like Google Classroom, and there is no one or "right" way to do that. Luckily many teachers share online their ideas, strategies, and innovative solutions. Here is an example of how Google Classroom is used by one teacher to reach students at their point.

3.3 Parent-Teacher Communication and Google Classroom

Google Classroom has ways for teachers to submit feedback on classroom research for students. However, it doesn't provide the degree of contact you'll find in applications Types include ClassDojo or Remind SeeSaw. Google refers to families and parents as "guardians" who can elect by email to receive summaries of incomplete assignments, upcoming assignments, and other class activity. Nevertheless, it does not provide apps for direct contact with families or permit families to comment on the work of their children.

3.4 Engaging and Interactive Content

Consider switching up the types of tools you share with them in Google Classroom to make learning with digital content more interactive for students. Aside from G Suite resources such as Google Docs and Google Slides, teachers and students can share other media forms, including photos, website links, YouTube videos, and screencasts.

Some teachers also have a range of choices for students to apply for their work inside Google Classroom. For example, you might give students an option to reply with a comment, video clip, or drawing to a reading assignment that demonstrates their thought.

When you are looking to build an interactive platform for students, you might be considering doing so on the Stream page of Google Classroom. The Stream is a feed inside Google Classroom where everyone in the class will find updates and upcoming assignments, and it is the first thing students see when they log in.

Some teachers use the Stream to set up class discussion boards, where students can connect online by asking questions or commenting on the posts. Such discussion boards will help improve class engagement and give more leverage to students in getting their voices heard (or read) by the teacher. You can use the Stream as a closed social network of sorts with conversations, and it can be a great way to help children practice using all kinds of different digital citizenship skills in a "walled garden" style environment.

Chapter 4: Reasons to Use Google Classroom

4.1 Benefits of Using Google Classroom

Google Classroom provides many opportunities for both students and teachers as a free online learning site. Here are ten reasons teachers should try it out.

Accessibility

Google Classroom can be accessed via Google Chrome from any machine, or from any mobile device, regardless of platform. All files shared by teachers and students shall be stored in a Classroom folder on Google Drive. Users can access the Classroom anywhere, anywhere. Students can't complain about broken machines or starving dogs anymore.

Exposure

The classroom offers access to an online learning program for the students. Many programs at the college and university now require students to participate in at least one online class. Google Classroom exposure can help students turn to other learning management systems used in higher education.

Paperless

Teachers and students won't have to shuffle excessive quantities of paper since the Classroom is entirely paperless. When teachers upload assignments and assessments to the Classroom, they are saved to drive simultaneously. Students can complete assignments and assessments directly via Classroom, and even keep their work to Drive. Students may access lost work due to absences and find other likely required services.

Time Saver

The classroom is a perfect time-saver. With all money being saved in one location and being able to access the Classroom anytime, teachers would have more free time to complete other tasks. As the Classroom is accessible from a mobile device, teachers and students can participate via their phones or tablets.

Communication

Teachers and students can submit emails, post into the web, submit private comments on assignments, and provide input on work. Teachers are in complete charge of comments and posts from the students. They can also connect with parents via individual emails or via email summaries from the Classroom that include class announcements and dates.

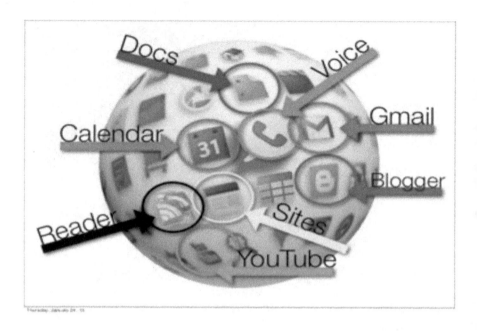

Collaborate

The classroom gives the students many ways to work together. Teachers will encourage online discussions inside the Classroom between students and build group projects. Additionally, students can collaborate on teacher shared Google Docs.

Engagement

Many digital natives are familiar with technology and would be more likely to use technology to take control of their learning. The classroom offers many ways to make learning collaborative and interactive.

It allows teachers to separate tasks, to incorporate videos and web pages into lessons, and to create group tasks for collaboration.

Differentiation

The teachers can easily distinguish instruction for learners via the Classroom. Assigning readings to the entire class, individual students, or student groups only takes a few necessary steps when making an assignment on the Classwork website.

Feedback

A valuable part of all learning is to provide meaningful feedback to the students. Inside the Classroom's grading tool, teachers can send feedback on assignments to each student. There's also the opportunity to build a comment bank for potential use inside the grading method. Additionally, the iOS app Classroom helps users to annotate research.

Data Analysis

To make learning meaningful, teachers should review evaluation data to ensure students recognize learning goals. Data from assessments can be conveniently exported for processing and analyzing into Sheets.

Google Classroom is a Workflow Management System.

Many learning management systems have many great features, including most of the features that Google Classroom provides. Still, the complexity of their feature sets can make them difficult to use and too complicated for teachers who are less technically confident. Content management systems are mainly designed to provide students with the knowledge, while missing many of the features teachers need, such as online assignments and grade books.

Ben believes that the great thing about Google Classroom is that it incorporates the best of all systems, making it something like a "workflow management framework," as he describes it. Google Classroom can be a significant first step for teachers looking to get started in a digital teaching environment by offering an easy, user-friendly forum for content sharing, assignments development, and grading.

Google Docs is a digital Xerox machine, with Google Classroom.

In a very practical way, Google Classroom makes it easier for teachers to work in the way it treats papers.

Normally, if a teacher decides to create a worksheet for her students, she will create it in a word processor, print it out, make photocopies, give it out to her students, hope no one loses it (which, of course, somebody still does), and then collect it when it's done.

The process is much more straightforward with Google Classroom. In Google Docs, the instructor simply generates the worksheet, shares it with her students, and then each student gets a personalized, editable copy of their own with a big blue turn-in button top. There is no printing, no photocopying, no job losses, and when students apply for their jobs, the instructor can also receive updates on her computer.

Google Classroom helps the teachers to have real-time input.

Google Docs has been an excellent interactive resource since well before Google Classroom came along; owing in large part to the way it enables multiple users to work on a single document at the same time. As Ben points out, this opportunity to see a colleague typing in real-time, when coupled with Google Classroom, can be an extremely useful resource for students.

Another example of this that Ben provides is that of a Spanish teacher who assigns a worksheet on Google Docs to their students and then sits on their computer and "jumps" into each of their assignments while they work on them. It helps her to watch the students carrying out their translations in real-time, and to give live feedback and suggestions on their work — a method that is often more difficult and distracting as it involves wandering around a classroom and peering over the heads of the students.

Google Classroom shines on the iPad.

In early 2015, Google released its iOS app for iPads, making it one of the most popular ways teachers can access and use the web ever since.

Although the app presents a strong mobile version of the standard features of Google Classroom, it shines in the way it blends the innovative capabilities of the iPad with the excellent organizational tools of Google Classroom.

In the Google Classroom app the professor will create the assignment correctly. Then the student will use apps to create the video. such as Animoto and iMovie, and with a few easy clicks, send the finished file directly to their instructor.

Whereas such a project would usually involve several computers, video cameras, and file storage devices, by integrating Google Classroom with the iPad, teachers can take it from assignment to production to assessment without using anything other than the iPad.

Google Classroom is easy to use.

Google Classroom is extremely easy when compared to other LMS (Learning Management Systems) that have been common over the past decade.

Our tech team practiced for about an hour, and by the end of the training, we had all set up and run a classroom.

Google Classroom is there to help you interact more effectively.

Only until you enter the students 'email addresses, and contact in the school is over. The instructor only has an email address, a discussion group, and automatically created a Google Calendar by joining the student in the classroom. And adding and removing students from class as needed is simple.

Google Classroom is designed to help you interact better.

The communication tools are probably more important than being easy to use and usable, but they are also beneficial.

Since it's all Cloud-based, students no longer "lose" assignments. The correspondence is smooth when a student is absent. Google Classroom just last month introduced a parent notification feature to keep parents updated on what's going on in the classroom.

Google Classroom is cost-effective and environmentally friendlier.

I'm not sold entirely on paperless learning, particularly for younger learners. Yet when it comes to copying and printing, I see a definite benefit for schools to be more cost-effective. Because every student already has a laptop that links to the Internet, every piece of paper we save can just make the school more productive and environmentally friendly.

That's how students can continue to learn in the future.

College campuses no longer require their five-page papers to be read by undergraduates. As K-12 educators, we will take notice of this and train our students for the world in which they will live. For students who struggle, it's easier as long as you help them handle the unit. The reason Google Classroom is better is because of its operational advantage.

Tasks never get lost, and the teacher is already planning every classroom. Navigating this has to be taught for these students, though. Although students are digital natives, this does not mean they understand how adults are arranging their environment to help them learn.

Collaboration outside of school (i.e., Flipped Classroom) is more straightforward with Google Classroom.

Again, with a link, it is Cloud-based and available from anywhere. Students are permitted to exchange assignments and work together from home to complete them. Collaboration isn't all about interacting with other peers in a group. An instructor will toggle around the classroom by uploading a video to go live at night, allowing students to watch it that night to practice for the next day's quiz. The possibilities are endless. Planning for teachers is easy, and it is worth the up-front time. In Google Classroom, more new features allow teachers to schedule future assignments. Designated assignments might be scheduled to go live in October on a Monday, and then close that Friday. Classrooms are also available from semester to semester and from year to year. Copying and pasting a lesson for the next group of students would be awful for an instructor, but it saves some time to have some items already in place (class syllabus, grading standards, etc.).

Feedback is instantaneous and functional by embedding the elements.

This improves interaction and transparency, which helps the instructor to see outcomes at the end of the lesson, too. If students struggled to respond with the correct answers, she could then cover the material again.

The enhancements and updates are constant.

This is one of Google Classroom's best-selling points for me, by far. Google actively listens and reacts if anything needs to be added or fixed (from this came both the timing of the assignment and the parent communication). That also means teachers will have to keep learning as they use it ... which is not a bad thing either!

Conclusion

Google Classroom is a free software program. Google Classroom helps teachers and students interact and can be used in the coordination and management of assignments, to go paperless, to work with students and teachers, to teach from afar, and so on! You could compare it to Showbiz, as well as other online learning platforms or management systems.

Google Docs and Google Drive have it installed on top, so any teacher will find it very easy and intuitive to use. This doesn't mean it's dull though. Google Classroom is filled with surprises you'll come across along the way. Reporting on originality allows educators and students to see the parts and sections of the submitted work that contain the exact or similar wording to that of another source. To students it illustrates insufficient quotation source materials and flags to help the student develop their learning. Teachers can also display the originality report, so they can check the academic integrity of the research submitted by the student. On G Suite for Education (free), teachers can turn on 3 assignments to report originality. This limitation is removed on G Suite for Education Enterprise (paid).

Classroom offers students the ability to archive lessons at the end of a term or year. When a course is archived, it is removed from the site and put in the Archived Classes area to help teachers preserve the structure of their current classes. Teachers and students will access it when a course is archived, but it won't be able to make any modifications until it's modified. The apps allow users to take images and add them to their assignments, transfer files from other applications, and offline access supports. Like Google's consumer services, Google Classroom, as part of G Suite for Education, does not display ads for students, faculty, and teachers in its app, and user data are not searched or used for advertising purposes. Google Classroom can be accessed via Google Chrome from any machine, or from any mobile device, regardless of platform. Classroom brings exposure to an online learning system for students. Teachers and students won't have to shuffle excessive quantities of paper since Classroom is completely paperless. Classroom is a perfect time-. Teachers and students can submit emails, post into the web, submit private comments on assignments, and provide input on work. Teachers are in complete charge of comments and posts from the students. They can also connect with parents via individual emails or via email summaries from Classroom that include class announcements and dates. Classroom gives the students many ways to work together. Teachers will encourage online discussions inside the Classroom between students and build group projects. Many digital natives are familiar with technology, and would be more likely to use technology to take control of their learning. Classroom offers many ways to make learning collaborative and interactive. It gives teachers the opportunity to separate tasks, to incorporate videos and web pages into lessons, and to create group tasks for collaboration.

References

- What Is Google Classroom? - dummies. Retrieved from **https://www.dummies.com/education/internet-basics/ what-is-google-classroom/**

- 50 Things You Can Do With Google Classroom - Teacher Tech. Retrieved from **https://alicekeeler.com/ 2015/05/11/50-things-you-can-do-with-google-classroom/**

- Classroom: manage teaching and learning | Google for Education. Retrieved from **http://classroom.google.com/**

- Google Classroom. Retrieved from **https:// en.wikipedia.org/wiki/Google_Class_room**

- Learning, T., Strategies, T., America, S., Plan?, W., Launches, S., & Education, T. et al. 10 Benefits of Google Classroom Integration - The Tech Edvocate. Retrieved from **https://www.thetechedvocate.org/10-benefits-of-google-classroom-integration/**

- Bielefeld, K. Ten Reasons Why You Should Use Google Classroom. Retrieved from **https://blog.mimio.com/ten-reasons-why-you-should-use-google-classroom**

- How to Create a Class in Google Classroom - dummies. Retrieved from **https://www.dummies.com/education/ internet-basics/how-to-create-a-class-in-google-classroom/**

- The beginners guide to Google Classroom. Retrieved from https://www.bookwidgets.com/blog/2017/05/the-beginners-guide-to-google-classroom

- Teachers' Essential Guide to Google Classroom | Common Sense Education. Retrieved from https://www.commonsense.org/education/articles/teachers-essential-guide-to-google-classroom

- 6 Great Google Classroom Tips for Teachers | Common Sense Education. Retrieved from https://www.commonsense.org/education/articles/6-great-google-classroom-tips-for-teachers